GREAT
PHILOSOPHERS

Consulting Editors
Ray Monk and Frederic Raphael

Gideon Calder

....

RORTY

And Redescription

Weidenfeld & Nicolson

LONDON

First published in Great Britain in 2003
by Weidenfeld & Nicolson

© 2003 Gideon Calder

A CIP catalogue record for this book
is available from the British Library.

ISBN 0 297 60754 5

Typeset by Deltatype Ltd, Birkenhead, Merseyside

Printed in Great Britain by Clays Ltd, St Ives plc

Weidenfeld & Nicolson

The Orion Publishing Group Ltd
Orion House
5 Upper Saint Martin's Lane
London, WC2H 9EA

For Arabella

RORTY

And Redescription

INTRODUCTION

From the start, philosophy has had a habit of giving birth to its own would-be gravediggers. This may be in the nature of the business. To 'big', ultimate questions the 'biggest', ultimate answer might seem to be that there *are* no answers – that it's the framing of the questions which is causing the trouble. Indeed, many key exponents of the last 150 years or so have insisted that philosophy is not the sort of practice which has a 'nature' in the first place: that neither in terms of subject-matter nor of technique is there anything constant, unique or necessary about the philosophical enterprise. This, in turn, irritates those who contend that explaining human existence is a matter of seeking absolutes – of finding a neutral framework, detached from the flux of history, by which to discern the nature of the world and our relationship to it.

Presented as an attempt to escape into an otherworldly realm of the eternally guaranteed, this purist picture has been readily flipped over and exposed as self-delusion. From Marx to Heidegger, and Beauvoir to Habermas, its modern critics have argued that to insist on the isolability of philosophical questions from the social, historical, interpretive or cultural backdrop against which they take on their significance – and indeed from the history of philosophy itself – is actually to render philosophy either theoretically untenable or critically toothless. In one sense,

Richard Rorty belongs to this philosophical counter-tradition (and indeed, this questionably clean division of philosophers into purists and historicists has a decidedly Rortian flavour). Yet in another, he does not. Unlike Marx or the French phenomenologists, Rorty does not seek to replace a loftily abstract model of critique with a version more concretely rooted in social relations, or in the realities of lived experience. Together with his objections to the urge to keep philosophy pure and ahistorical, comes a suspicion of theorising *as such*. This book tries to explain that suspicion, and to outline Rorty's suggestions as to how we might do without theory altogether. His work, it should be noted at the start, is full of polemical reductions and tactical swerves; at every point there are claims and moves to be questioned or unpacked. This caution granted, the intention here is to go with its flow, and save quibbles for the later stages.

Rorty was born in 1931, the only son of Trotskyist activists, and grew up in New York and New Jersey before leaving for the University of Chicago at the age of fifteen. He read for a PhD at Yale, and has since taught at Wellesley College, at Princeton, at the University of Virginia and currently at Stanford, where he is Professor of Comparative Literature. His work is probably cited as much and as widely as any contemporary philosopher writing in English. *Philosophy and the Mirror of Nature*, the book which mostly made his name, was recently counted among the *Times Literary Supplement*'s hundred most influential books in any field since the Second World War.[1] But this notoriety has seen no simple translation into wide esteem or iconic status – at least, not among philosophers. There is no Rortian school, as such. Rorty-*bashing*, however, is something of a sunrise industry in various circles. A renegade to purists, a reactionary to radicals, and a subversive to conservatives, his major intellectual allegiance is to the American pragmatist tradition – most particularly, to the legacy of John Dewey (1859–1952). Yet even other self-proclaimed pragmatists tend to view him with suspicion. Meanwhile he presents his ideas as the culmination and extension of many of the most familiar and fashionable trends in contemporary thinking.

As we'll see, there are good reasons to react to Rorty's thinking with scepticism and unease. But a dominant factor in the reception history of his work among philosophers is, on the face of it, rather less impressive. It's a certain disciplinary defensiveness, in response to a key aspect of Rorty's approach. As far as he himself is concerned he is not 'doing' philosophy, but rather drawing attention to a certain gap between what philosophers think philosophy is, and what it actually amounts to, or is good for. His work is steeped in, and often explicitly parasitic on, the history of philosophy. But it looks at that history synoptically, as an episode. Rorty spins another narrative as a sort of sequel to a drama, Philosophy, which, with changes in *dramatis personae* and the occasional shift of plot, has run and run since Socrates, but which – partly due to the implications of some of its own most important developments – has recently been losing momentum. Rorty's typical rhetorical strategy is to set up an opposition between different sides of some key philosophical debate and then demonstrate why the core problem that divides them is not really a problem at all. One Rorty-endorsed name for this sort of approach is 'redescription'.

'Redescription' is a useful 'way in' to Rorty's work – and is the theme of this book – for two main reasons. Firstly, his work itself is a redescription of the nature and scope of philosophical thinking, and inquiry in general. He has spent most of his career, from his earliest published works of the late 1950s onwards, disputing stubborn aspects of Philosophy's self-image: the notion that there are correct ways of representing reality in words or in thought, and the notion, as he puts it, that we could possibly know in advance 'the terms in which all possible problems are to be set, and the criteria for their resolution' (CP, 109) – and present these terms in a language which is somehow universal, or transparent. The idea that philosophy might provide such terms and such a language rests upon another: that there is a way of thinking theoretically, distinct in its concerns and in its methodological approach to them, which somehow 'reaches deeper' than the rest of culture, to a special level of profundity. This in turn presupposes that there is an important metaphysical distinction between the appearance of things – their human-relative aspect – and their intrinsic, non-human reality. This distinction under-girds the very idea that 'theory' might progress either by abstraction from features of everyday experience to their preconditions, or by penetrating beneath the veil of mere appearances to their root material causes. From cultural theorists who insist that truth is 'really' inseparable from power, to the jobbing chemist conducting lab experiments, this idea still lurks naggingly in intellectual drives and mission-statements.

In Plato's famous simile of the cave in *The Republic*, the idea of a deeper reality beyond the everyday world of mediated appearances is given its classic articulation.[2] Rorty suggests that this appearance/reality distinction is defunct, having led philosophy – especially the analytic variety predominant in Britain and America – up a succession of blind alleys, and left it dealing with an entirely disposable agenda of pseudo-problems connected with how it is that things like words and mental states and objects in the world relate to one another. These problems are products of – and are problems only in terms of – a certain 'vocabulary', or way of speaking. This vocabulary can be traced back to the idea that to be rational we somehow need to make contact with, and find a way of representing, the way the world, by itself, non-humanly, *is*. This misbegotten hope comes as a package with the appearance/reality distinction, and its positing of a *real* world beyond the dark confines in which the unenlightened are kept prisoner. For Rorty, that distinction can be costlessly replaced with a rather lower-key alternative: between more or less useful descriptions of the world.

Hence the second significance of redescription. Rorty's alternative to philosophy as traditionally conceived is to substitute ongoing redescription of our circumstances and horizons for the gradual unveiling of their 'real' nature. In place of seeing inquiry as a progression along a pre-established line towards truer understanding, Rorty sees it as a process of putting ideas in different contexts, and coming up with novel descriptions. It is in terms of this model that he accounts for social and scientific progress, and for the progression of Western culture towards more liberal and inclusive social institutions and practices. Thus he has no interest in supplanting one theoretical approach by the greater force of another, or indeed in proffering what purist philosophers would regard as 'proper arguments', honouring accepted logical maxims. Preference for the latter depends on an assumption that in some sense, philosophy seeks an anchor, first principles, a foundation which itself requires no foundation, on the basis of which all further answers are to be derived. This search for the *a priori*, the timeless starting-point for all inquiry – sometimes called 'foundationalism' – might have kept philosophers entertained for millennia. But it hasn't succeeded, and is losing its attraction:

> Interesting philosophy is rarely an examination of the pros and cons of a thesis. Usually it is, implicitly or explicitly, a contest between an entrenched vocabulary which has become a nuisance and a half-formed new vocabulary which vaguely promises great things. The latter 'method' of philosophy is the same as the 'method' of utopian politics or revolutionary science (as opposed to parliamentary politics, or normal science). The method is to redescribe lots and lots of things in new ways, until you have created a pattern of linguistic

behavior which will tempt the rising generation to adopt it, thereby causing them to look for appropriate new forms of nonlinguistic behavior, for example, the adoption of new scientific equipment or new social institutions. This sort of philosophy does not work piece by piece, analyzing concept after concept, or testing thesis after thesis. Rather, it works holistically and pragmatically. It says things like 'try thinking of it this way' – or more specifically, 'try to ignore the apparently futile traditional philosophical questions by substituting the following new and possibly interesting questions'. (CIS, 9)

An appeal to logic, rigour and precision as eternal 'rules' by which claims on our attention are to be evaluated is replaced by an appeal to narrative – through which, without such limits or foundations, 'we live in story after story after story' (FPPP, 2).

Put differently, though one *can* think of philosophy purely as a sort of collaborative, 'scientific' project of deductive system-building,

one can also think of philosophy in other ways – in particular, as a matter of telling stories: stories about why we talk as we do and how we might avoid continuing to talk that way. When you find yourself at an argumentative impasse, baffled by your opponent's refusal to stop asking questions which you think you really should not have to answer, you can always shift the ground by raising questions about the vocabulary he or she is using. You can point out that the issue is biased

9

> in one's opponent's favour by the unfortunate jargon
> which has developed, a jargon which gives one's
> opponent an unfair advantage. (PP, 461)

There are no pre-given criteria for such story-telling, no in-built requirements or constraints (derived from logic, or our own nature as human subjects, or that of language). Neither, *a fortiori*, is there anything about the world we describe which limits or pronounces upon the stories we tell about it. The world does not intervene in our stories. It does not choose which among the descriptions we make of it will be successful. We approach the world from within any one among a choice of vocabularies, or (to use Wittgenstein's term) language games, none of which is closer or closest to the way the world actually is.

> But the realization that the world does not tell us which
> language games to play should not, however, lead us to
> say that a decision about which to play is arbitrary, nor
> to say that it is the expression of something deep within
> us. The moral is not that objective criteria for choice of
> vocabulary are to be replaced with subjective criteria,
> reason with will or feeling. It is rather that the notions of
> criteria and choice (including that of 'arbitrary' choice)
> are no longer in point when it comes to changes from
> one language game to another. Europe did not *decide* to
> accept the idiom of Romantic poetry, or of socialist
> politics, or of Galilean mechanics. That sort of shift was
> no more an act of will than it was a result of argument.
> Rather, Europe gradually lost the habit of using certain

words and gradually acquired the habit of using new ones . . . What was glimpsed at the end of the eighteenth century was that anything can be made to look good or bad, important or unimportant, useful or useless, by being redescribed. (CIS, 6–7)

Rorty's contention here is that competing descriptions of the world are, argumentatively speaking, all we have. Nothing about the world is going to declare itself in favour of any given one of them, as if there was a prize to be won from 'the nature of things' when we finally hit upon its single true description. Rather, different descriptions, framed within different vocabularies, simply 'help us see' (to use a favourite phrase of Rorty's) given fields of inquiry in different ways. Things are out there, certainly, separate from our descriptions – but it is only our descriptions which can be true or false, compelling or repulsive, acceptable or unacceptable. 'Only descriptions of the world can be true or false. The world on its own – unaided by the describing activities of human beings – cannot.' (CIS, 5)

Now many others besides have argued that, because of the nature and scope of language, what we really talk about in philosophy, or science, is our own descriptions rather than the world itself. A shift in the direction of language as in some sense prior to other considerations has occurred in various forms of thinking since the late 1800s. For Kant, one of philosophy's first tasks was to demonstrate how it is that our thoughts link up with sense experience: how it is, for instance, that we apply the concept 'dog' to a brown furry thing lolloping down the stairs towards us. Kant's answer was, roughly, that the very orderliness of our everyday experience presupposes an underlying unity to thought – a formal, universal order of faculties which dictates the nature of the way in which the world appears to us. Since then, much of philosophy has taken a 'linguistic turn'. It has focused on the fact that, as well as being a concept, 'dog' is a piece of language: a piece of language which seems to have a crucial mediating role between our thoughts and our experience of the world.

This adds an extra dimension to epistemology as Kant conceived it: we cannot move straight from the world to our ideas of it, bypassing the way in which those ideas are expressed. Instead, we must treat language as thoroughly implicated in the knowledge process. From the structuralist linguistics of Saussure to the hermeneutic phenomenology of Heidegger, from Frege to Chomsky, philosophers and linguists have grappled with the question of the relation of thought to language, and assumed more and more that the traditional order of logical priority between the two (that we speak language) might be reversed: that language, in an important sense, speaks us. Many now claim that the workings of language are a sort of preconditional fabric for our individual, apparently spontaneous, claims and utterances making sense – and for there being a 'world' to which discourse relates. Rorty goes along with this up to a point, agreeing that our awareness of the world is in some sense a linguistic affair. But he resists the idea (key, for instance, to Frege's thinking) that what philosophy must now do is identify the preconditions for our statements about the world (as opposed to our ideas of it) making sense. Rorty's point is that there is nothing intrinsic about language, no system of conditions, which makes our descriptions meaningful. Theory of language does not provide any more weighty an anchor than anything else:

> Philosophy of language, done in the manner of Frege, was supposed to produce conditions of describability, just as Kant had promised to produce conditions of experienceability. Describability, like experienceability, was supposed to be the mark of everything studied or exemplified by all areas of study other than philosophy. Language seemed able to avoid relativization to history, for description was thought to be a single indissoluble activity, whether done by Neanderthals, Greeks, or Germans. If one could give *a priori* conditions of the activity of description, then one would be in a position to offer apodeictic truths. (EHO, 54)

We can't. Recent philosophers have helped us to appreciate

> the power of redescribing, the power of language to make new and different things possible and important – an appreciation which becomes possible only when one's aim becomes an expanding repertoire of alternative descriptions rather than The One Right Description. (CIS, 39–40)

For Rorty, then, it is descriptions themselves which furnish the horizons of inquiry. But if this is so, why did philosophers take so long to realise it?

THE TROUBLE WITH EPISTEMOLOGY

It took so long because, since its inception, professional-ised philosophy in the Western world has been embarked upon a concerted project the presuppositions of which are fundamentally awry.

We have gathered that Rorty has spent most of his career trying to debunk any lingering idea on the part of philosophers, especially analytical philosophers, that their discipline is one, as he puts it, 'that will (any day now) produce noncontroversial results concerning matters of ultimate concern' (ORT, 75) – a discipline which suppos-edly 'discovers', 'reveals', 'represents', or 'reflects' underly-ing realities about human beings and their relation to the world and each other. As Rorty maps it out in *Philosophy and the Mirror of Nature*, the story of modern philosophy is the story of the consolidation of this unfortunate self-image. It is a story in which 'philosophy' becomes, in intellectual circles, a substitute for religion as the place to go to find 'the vocabulary and the convictions which [permit] one to explain and justify one's activity as an intellectual, and thus to discover the significance of one's life' (PMN, 4).

Philosophy and the Mirror of Nature makes a narrative of philosophical themes and variations since the 1600s. 'The aim of the book,' as it says near the start, is to undermine the reader's confidence in 'the mind' as something about which one should have a 'philosophical' view, in 'knowledge' as something about which there ought to be a 'theory' and which has 'foundations', and in 'philosophy' as it has been conceived since Kant.

It is pictures rather than propositions, metaphors rather than statements, which determine most of our philosophical convictions. The picture which holds traditional philosophy together is that of the mind as a great mirror, containing various representations – some accurate, some not – and capable of being studied by pure, nonempirical methods. Without the notion of the mind as mirror, the notion of knowledge as accuracy of representation would not have suggested itself. (PMN, 7, 12)

Whence did this picture of the mind arrive? Modern philosophy is commonly taken to have been launched by René Descartes' *Meditations* (1641), its approach epitomised by the famous passage in which the sceptical Descartes sits down with his thoughts by the fireside and sets out systematically to doubt every aspect of his apparent awareness of external objects. In search of a truth unable to be doubted, Descartes finally hits upon the ground below which he cannot further fall: his own consciousness. He may be dreaming each experience; his every sensation might be 'illusions and deceptions' by which some 'evil demon' is trying to delude him. But even to be so deceived, he must be *thinking*, and here at last is his piece of certainty:

'*I am*, *I exist*, is necessarily true, every time I express it or conceive of it in my mind.'[3] So begins a story, a story which posits a separate mental realm, separate from the world of physical bodies, which is somehow responsible for what is crucial about us as human beings and, most importantly, is crucial to what we can *know*. This picture is the by-product of an imaginative thought-experiment, a figurative device. But the picture sticks.

On the basis of this quirk of happenstance, a philosophical agenda is set. This agenda is responsible for, among other things, several centuries' worth of debates between rationalists and empiricists on the provenance of knowledge; worryings about which if any among our ideas might be 'clear and distinct', and so foundational; fallings-out over whether the world is 'fundamentally' ideal or material. Rorty is not the first to argue that all these things – staple stuff in first-year undergraduate philosophy syllabuses – hinge on this positing of a radical gap between 'I' and 'it', between subject and object, or the mind as mirror and the thing (nature) which it mirrors. But his redescription of philosophy as 'captive to a picture' presents a catalogue of reasons – mostly gleaned from the development of thinking since Descartes – why that picture might be difficult to sustain.

Specifically, his case seems to undermine the idea that the world might have an intrinsic or hidden nature to be represented, that the Truth is something to be revealed by the world to the most convincing theoretical bidder. If we think that it is, then this is a hangover from seventeenth-

and eighteenth-century conceptions of mind and knowledge, and the idea that the Truth – the way the world 'really is' – is something to be attained by meticulous attention to the rationality of the ways in which we apply our minds or language to the world. A suitably polished mirror duly reflects, and a suitably exact language represents, nature's own chosen self-image – or so tradition has it:

> To take the traditional idea of Truth seriously, you have to do more than agree that some beliefs are true and some false, and to call 'true' those which fit best with your and others' previous beliefs. . . . To respect Truth and Reality in the proper way, it is not enough to come in when it rains, and to shun bears. To acquire the right sort of respect, it helps if you can manage to become an epistemological sceptic – manage to worry about whether human language is capable of representing the way Reality is in itself, whether we are calling Reality by the names it prefers. To worry in this way, you need to take seriously the question whether our descriptions of reality may not be all too human, all too influenced by our hopes and fears. It helps to anguish about whether Reality (and therefore Truth itself) may not stand aloof, beyond the reach of the sentences in which we formulate our beliefs. You must be prepared to distinguish, at least in principle, between beliefs which embody Truth and beliefs which are merely good to steer by. (SSB, 7)

Among other things, such worries are responsible for the fear of 'relativism' – the thesis that what counts as truth, far from being *absolute* or universal, is only ever *relative* to the language one speaks, one's perspective, one's cultural circumstances, or whatever else. Rorty thinks you can avoid these worries by allying yourself to the pragmatist conclusion that, in the words of William James, 'the true is the name of whatever proves itself to be good in the way of belief'.[4] Being 'good to steer by' does not imply any sort of direct correspondence to the way things 'really are': it simply means that the truth, in the most generalistic classification we can find, is what *works*.

'Essentialist' philosophers, in the tradition of Descartes' radical separation of mind and external world, insist on fundamental oppositions, between which it is philosophy's task to build a fail-safe bridge. Anti-essentialists, on the other hand, insist that all of these are hangovers from the urge to divide the world according to the dualistic metaphors of Plato and Descartes:

> The anti-essentialist philosopher looks forward to the day when all the pseudo-problems created by the essentialist tradition – problems about the relation of appearance to reality, of mind to body, of language to fact – will be dissolved. She thinks that all these traditional dualisms collapse, like so many dominoes, once the distinction between essence and accident is collapsed. She sees the distinction between reality and appearance as a way of suggesting that some set of relations, some context, is intrinsically privileged. She sees the mind-body distinction as a way of suggesting that human beings have an inside which is beyond the reach of language, or possess

> an intrinsic intentionality, a kind which escapes recon-
> textualization. She sees the distinction between lan-
> guage and fact as a way of intimating that some bits of
> language bear a special relation – that of accurate
> representation – to something which is what it is apart
> from language, apart from any description. (ORT, 99)

What Rorty means here is perhaps best explained by way of
his frequent invocation of another metaphor: what the
contemporary American philosopher Donald Davidson
calls the 'scheme-content distinction'.[5] This is the 'presumption that there is some sort of inviolable "metaphysical" break between the formal and the material, the
logical and the psychological, the non-natural and the
natural' (ORT, 168). This distinction arises in all sorts of
forms, but is responsible for most of the core issues in
courses called 'Introduction to Philosophy' – questions like
'Can we defeat the problem of sceptical doubt?' and 'Is the
world fundamentally ideal or material?' To Rorty, these are
pseudo-questions thrown up by a particular habit of
thinking which drives a wedge between culture and nature,
or what we *think* and what *is*, or the way we describe
ourselves and the way we 'really are', or contingent
constructions and what is necessary and given. Like most
bad habits, this can be dispensed with without any great
loss:

> if we once adopt the 'scheme-content' distinction – the
> distinction between determinate realities and a set of
> words or concepts which may or may not be 'adequate'
> to them – we shall, needlessly, find ourselves worried

about relativism-vs.-absolutism – about whether our knowledge is merely 'relative' to what [Bernard] Williams calls 'our perspective and its peculiarities' or whether it is in touch with what [David] Lewis calls 'objective sameness and difference in nature'. So he urges that we drop that distinction, and with it the notion that beliefs represent a content according to the conventions of a scheme. Davidson . . . does not think that . . . any natural science . . . can provide a skyhook – something which might lift us out of our beliefs to a standpoint from which we glimpse the relations of those beliefs to reality. Rather, he takes us to be in touch with reality in all areas of culture – ethics as well as physics, literary criticism as well as biology – in a sense of 'in touch with' which does not mean 'representing reasonably accurately' but simply 'caused by and causing'. (ORT, 9)

We'll return in the next section to what Rorty means by 'caused by and causing'. In the meantime, it suffices to notice the gist of his case so far. The idea that 'truth' (for instance) might be a theoretical problem is simply the product of an approach which assumes that there is a bedrock reality in relation to which different approaches, different disciplines, come more or less close, and are more or less accurate. An example of this would be the realist assumption that a scientific theory that works must have hit upon something *independently* true about the world. To this picture of a self-contained, constant world about which our contingent descriptions will be more or less accurate Rorty opposes a 'historicist' version:

In a historicist account, there is no description either of nature or of experience that is more or less accurate or concrete than some rival (unless 'more accurate' and 'more concrete' are construed pragmatically, as 'more useful for the following purposes . . .'). (RP, 4)

Unlike 'realists', who wish to ground solidarity in objectivity, those who wish to reduce objectivity to solidarity – call them 'pragmatists' – do not require either a metaphysics or an epistemology. They view truth as, in William James's phrase, what is good for *us* to believe. . . . For pragmatists, the desire for objectivity is not the desire to escape the limitations of one's community, but simply the desire for as much intersubjective agreement as possible, the desire to extend the reference of 'us' as far as we can. . . . If we could be moved solely by the desire for solidarity, setting aside the desire for objectivity altogether, then we should think of human progress as making it possible for human beings to do more interesting things and be more interesting people, not as heading towards a place which has somehow been prepared for us in advance. (ORT, 22–3, 27)

Not only are scientists not 'revealing' anything about the way the world antecedently 'is', but, by extension, neither are those who would unmask the 'real' nature of *anything*, be it our own humanity, or patriarchy, or historical events, or the meaning of *As I Lay Dying*. For any such project of 'unmasking' relies precisely upon those same, old, tired-out metaphors:

without the traditional concepts of metaphysics one cannot make sense of the appearance-reality distinction, and without that distinction one cannot make sense of the notion of 'what is really going on'. No more metaphysics, no more unmasking. (DP, 14)

This unfortunate picture of human inquiry gradually unmasking the reality behind appearances is built into all Plato-esque eschatologies of humanity's progression from ignorance towards enlightenment:

The urge to tell stories of progress, maturation and synthesis might be overcome if we once took seriously the notion that we only know the world and ourselves *under a description* – and that we just *happened on* that description – nature didn't tell us to apply it, it didn't best unify the manifold of previous descriptions, we just *chanced* onto it. (FE, 48)

We should, then, replace the aim of 'unmasking' an underlying reality with something which denies the need for any hard-and-fast account of what counts as knowledge, or what it is good for:

If we see knowing not as having an essence, to be described by scientists or philosophers, but rather as a right, by current standards, to believe, then we are well on the way to seeing *conversation* as the ultimate context within which knowledge is to be understood. (PMN, 389)

This accepted, we can accept too that there is nothing

about the world or about ourselves which provides neces-sary rules or ultimate constraints on our descriptions of the world:

> there are no constraints on inquiry save conversational ones – no wholesale constraints derived from the nature of objects, or of the mind, or of language, but only those retail constraints provided by the remarks of our fellow inquirers. (CP, 165)

> To see keeping a conversation going as a sufficient aim of philosophy, to see wisdom as consisting in the ability to sustain a conversation, is to see human beings as generators of new descriptions rather than beings one hopes to be able to describe accurately. (PMN, 377)

Rather than seeking 'a way of making further redescription unnecessary by finding a way of reducing all *possible* descriptions to one', the point is to keep the conversation going: to encourage ongoing redescription rather than to find objective truth (PMN, 377).

We must, then, stop imagining that we know ourselves, or anything else, 'except under optional descriptions' (PMN, 379), and moreover that any of those descriptions reaches 'deeper down' than the others, to the way things are in themselves. 'Down' is, in Rorty-speak, a particularly appropriate metaphorical usage. For a definitive, arguably *the* definitive, theme of his work (right from early 1960, when he first, in passing, makes the distinction) involves a contrast between *vertical* and *horizontal* inquiry. Vertical claims are those which posit some relation (for instance, 'representation') between an idea or a piece of language and an entity assumed to exist on a different ontological level: God, perhaps, or 'the way the world really is'. Epistemology as traditionally conceived is, for Rorty, sodden with such assumptions. Horizontal claims avoid any appeal to differentiated ontological levels. They refer only to other, preceding ideas or sentences. Indeed, with a suitably 'horizontalised' perspective, we will realise that there is no descriptive access – and no practical use in seeking to refer – to a separate 'reality' from that bequeathed to us by the horizons of previous descriptions and redescriptions. (On this contrast between the vertical and the horizontal, see PCL, 219–20.) The trick for Rorty, then, will be to explain what 'description' actually means, if not the description of a necessary, 'real' world by contingently existing, situated human beings.

A LANGUAGE FOR COPING

Few people not on hallucinogenic drugs have ever seriously suggested that there is any simple relation of identity between the very form of the word 'turnip' and the root vegetable to which the name refers. In themselves, the letters 't', 'u', 'r', 'n', 'i' and 'p', and the sounds they make, have nothing whatsoever to do with things eaten mashed up with haggis – and neither, for that matter, does the German *die Rübe* or the French *navet*. From this angle, the relation between the word that names and the object named seems purely arbitrary.

But still, words seem to refer to real things in the language-independent world. Language seems to *represent* – whether the thing represented is our own thoughts, or the aspect of the world which the sentence we utter is attempting to describe. The sounds and shapes of 'porridge' may have no resemblance to what I had for breakfast, but the word can (I hope) do the work required to convey my current breakfast-eating habits. More than that: my successful interaction with the world relies upon my separation of the word from its referent. Eating my words is not, however regular my *faux pas*, the source of much nutrition. To this extent, the word 'porridge' must refer directly to something beyond itself: there does indeed seem to be some connection, or fit, between word and object, designator and designated. How does this reference work? From Frege to Kripke, analytic philosophers have produced various explanations – perhaps, as in Frege's case, in terms of the meaning of the name itself (as supplying the criterion by which we identify what the word 'porridge' refers to), or, as Kripke would have it, of an original, 'reference-fixing' gesture by which the object is dubbed and the name is transferred through subsequent dialogue.

Emphasis in such explanations tends to settle either on the logic of language itself (and thus, since language is a human construct, on the role of our own intentions), or on the empirically grounded social practice of naming. Put differently, they start either with a name or with its object and draw (as it were) explanatory arrows to the other, showing the direction of the determinate relation between the two. As another example, the earlier work of Wittgenstein (in the *Tractatus Logico-Philosophicus*) argued that language 'pictures' the world, such that each sentence, even by itself, constitutes a sort of model of the state of affairs it represents.

But others have argued against the whole presumption that there must be some kind of substantial third factor linking language and world – a factor (called 'picturing', or 'reference', or whatever) which it is the job of philosophers of language to pin down and theorise. Saussure, famously, 'bracketed' the referential aspect of language altogether, arguing that the meaning of 'porridge' depends not on its relation to oats and water but on its differential relations to other signs within the same linguistic system. Look up a word you don't know in a dictionary or a thesaurus, and see how you discern its meaning: it is other words and concepts (taken together, 'signs'), Saussure would claim, which – by being more or less proximate, by not meaning the same thing – define a given name, rather than its relation to an object external to language.

Rorty's own position shares Saussure's anti-essentialism about the relation between word and object:

> The significance of a sentence, like that of a belief or a desire, is its place in a web of other sentences, or beliefs or desires. To say this is to emphasize the context-sensitivity of signs and of thoughts – to treat them not as quasi-things but as nodes in a web of relations. But that

is simply to describe them as antiessentialists wish *everything* – tables, quarks, people, social institutions – to be described. (EHO, 130–1)

Good anti-essentialists, then, insist that nothing (legs, turnips, the word 'combustion') means anything, or is describable, in isolation. They are *holists*: against the early Wittgenstein, they insist that all entities – including sentences and the objects they describe – exist only relationally. Individual words or sentences do not anatomically pick out, picture, or in any way lock onto the aspect of the world to which they refer, as if in a relation of direct correspondence. Rorty takes sentences rather than individual signs as the units of meaning, but for him as for Saussure, our understanding of language depends on having an interpretive context – a backdrop against which we make sense of the descriptions we come across.

But Rorty goes further, removing all suggestion of a 'systematic', structural aspect to language at all. As well as denying any direct relation between word and object, Rorty maintains that there is *nothing* (about the workings of language, the world, or a third, intervening force) which constrains the meaning of the sentences we utter other than the contingent context in which we utter them. The language we use, he argues, does not 'express' something from deep within us, nor 'represent' the world behind our immediate circumstances. It is not a *medium*, bridging internal thoughts and the external world at large, or indeed any kind of force with a complex or abstractly definable nature of its own. Rather, sentences are simply 'strings of marks and noises used by human beings in the development and pursuit of social practices' (LT, 373).

This picture of language is derived largely from that found in Wittgenstein's later *Philosophical Investigations*, where he famously likens language to a *tool*: 'Think of the tools in a tool-box: there is a hammer, pliers, a saw, a screwdriver, a rule, a glue-pot, glue, nails and screws. – The functions of words are as diverse as the functions of these objects.'[6] Tools have a meaning only in so far as they are used for particular, contingent purposes. There is no *overall* purpose for language, nor any definitive system within which the different tools fulfil their different mechanical roles. The function of words, for Rorty as for the Wittgenstein of the *Investigations*, depends upon the context in which we use those words: the specific 'language-game', or 'vocabulary' (to use Rorty's preferred term) within which we happen to be working at the time. It's not just that the vocabulary of astrology is seperate from that of rocket science in terms of their respective ontological assumptions. Rather, it's that ontology – or adequacy to an independently existing world – drops out of the picture altogether. Once one has rejected what Dewey called the 'spectator theory of knowledge' – and the assumption that the world itself has the sort of intrinsic nature which might be better viewed from some metaphysical vantage points than others – one will realise that

it is useless to ask whether one vocabulary rather than another is closer to reality. For different vocabularies serve different purposes, and there is no such thing as a

28

purpose that is closer to reality than another purpose. In particular, there is no purpose that is simply 'finding out how things are' as opposed to finding out how to predict their motion, explain their behaviour, and so on. . . . Nothing is conveyed by saying . . . that the vocabulary in which we predict the motion of a planet is more in touch with how things really are than the vocabulary in which we assign the planet an astrological influence. For to say that astrology is out of touch with reality cannot *explain* why astrology is useless; it merely restates that fact in misleading representationalist terms. (PAR, 3)

There is no big mystery to solve – no goal called Truth waiting at the end of inquiry to which successive or different vocabularies might, bit by bit, bring us closer. Neither is there any corresponding 'God's-eye view' (in Hilary Putnam's phrase) from which we might judge how close a given vocabulary is to reaching the goal. These alternative vocabularies are, argues Rorty, 'more like alternative tools than like bits of a jigsaw puzzle'. Thinking that they might be the latter suggests that vocabularies might 'be reducible to other vocabularies, or capable of being united with all other vocabularies in one grand unified super vocabulary' (CIS, 11) – in other words, that we might steadily progress towards a complete description of an antecedently existing nature of the world, rather than just different descriptions of the world.

A complete description would presuppose, of course, precisely that there is such an intrinsic nature of the world, to which our descriptions can be more or less accurate –

'that objects will constrain us to believe the truth about them, if only they are approached with an unclouded mental eye, or a rigorous method, or a perspicuous language' (CP, 165). Against this, Rorty insists that there is no description-independent 'way the world is'. Along with the rejection of the appearance/reality distinction must go that lingering assumption of the philosophical tradition which has seen

> language as interposed, like a cushion, between us and the world. . . . [I]f that metaphor goes, so does the traditional notion of an ideal language, or of the ideal empirical theory, as an ultrathin cushion which translates the brutal thrust of reality into statement and action as directly as possible. . . . The metaphors which the pragmatist suggests we put in [its] place . . . are those of linguistic behaviour as tool-using, of language as a way of grabbing hold of causal forces and making them do what we want, altering ourselves and our environment to suit our aspirations. (ORT, 81)

Thus language can't be accurate or wrong, mirror clearly or distort, because language is not a medium of representation. There is nothing general to be said about how words relate to the world. Language is simply an exchange of marks and noises, carried out in order to achieve specific purposes. We should drop altogether the ocularities to which 'spectator theories of knowledge' lead us – the hope that there is a sort of 'seeing clearly' which language might achieve, and that this is knowledge. For Rorty, there is no distinction to be had between knowing things and using them, or describing them for our own, contingent, particular purposes. An unflinching *nominalism* commits him to the view that generalities and patterns in the world are products of our own descriptions rather than of an independent order of things. For it is as instruments for purposes that our descriptions should be evaluated: 'Nominalists see language as just human beings using marks and noises to get what they want. One of the things we want to do with language is to get food, another is to get sex, another is to understand the origin of the universe' (EHO, 127). Getting the facts 'right', in this sense, 'is merely propaedeutic to finding a new and more interesting way of expressing ourselves, and thus of coping with the world' (PMN, 359).

To summarise this view of language – and consequently knowledge – as ways of 'coping with the world':

(1) language is not a medium between human subjects and worldly objects;
(2) all our awareness is under a description: the mind does not have immediate access to the world;
(3) all our descriptions are functions of social needs, so
(4) 'nature' and 'reality' in themselves are strictly beyond the scope of our description.

It follows from this that the intrinsic 'nature' of 'reality', being undescribable, is thereby also unknowable, and that 'truth' is not a relation between that nature and anything else:

we shall never be able to step outside of language, never

be able to grasp reality unmediated by a linguistic description. So both are ways of saying that we should be suspicious of the Greek distinction between appearance and reality, and that we should try to replace it with something like the distinction between 'less useful description of the world' and 'more useful description of the world'. . . . If you put the two slogans together, you get the claim that all our knowledge is under descriptions suited to our current social purposes. (PSH, 48)

It is, then, 'our current social purposes' which provide the anchor which grounds our claims, or the yardstick which assesses the utility of our descriptions. The only 'special' role that the acquisition of language plays in the development of such purposes is 'to let us enter a community whose members exchange justifications of assertions, and other actions, with each other' (PMN, 185). Pragmatists, having dropped that whole captivating picture of a mind trying to get in touch with a reality outside itself, can

start with a Darwinian account of human beings as animals doing their best to cope with the environment – doing their best to develop tools which will enable them to enjoy more pleasure and less pain. Words are among the tools which these clever animals have developed. There is no way in which tools can take one out of touch with reality. No matter whether the tool is a hammer or a gun or a belief or a statement, tool-using is part of the interaction of the organism with its environment. To see the employment of words as the use of tools to deal with the environment, rather than as an attempt to represent the intrinsic nature of that environment, is to repudiate the question of whether human minds are in touch with reality – the question asked by the epistemological sceptic. No organism, human or non-human, is ever more or less in touch with reality than any other organism. (PSH, xxiii)

What does this mean, though? Are objects invented by us? Are they just artefacts of language? Is nature simply a product of culture? Was there nothing to be talked about before people began talking? Is Rorty a *linguistic idealist*, someone who claims that there were no objects before language came along, that the world is simply the way we say it is, a product of our descriptions? Does he mean that the invention of the word 'tree' somehow, like God in *Genesis* saying 'Let there be light', created trees out of nothing? He says not:

none of us antirepresentationalists have ever doubted that most things in the universe are causally independent of us. What we question is whether they are representationally independent of us. For *X* to be representationally independent of us is for *X* to have an intrinsic feature (a feature that it has under any and every description) such that it is better described by some of our terms rather than others. Because we can see no way to decide which descriptions of an object get at what is 'intrinsic' to it, as opposed to its merely 'relational', extrinsic features (e.g., its description-relative features), we are prepared to discard the intrinsicextrinsic distinction, the claim that beliefs represent, and the whole question of representational independence or dependence. This means discarding the idea of . . . 'how things are *anyway*', apart from whether or how they are described. . . .

Take dinosaurs. Once you describe something as a dinosaur, its skin colour and sex life are causally independent of your having so described it. But before you describe it as a dinosaur, or as anything else, there is no sense to the claim that it is 'out there' having properties. *What* is out there? The thing-in-itself? The world? Tell us more. Describe it in more detail. Once you have done so, but only then, are we in a position to tell you which of its features are causally independent of having been so described and which are not. (TP, 86, 87)

The worry about linguistic idealism is based, Rorty claims, on a confusion between two separate questions. One concerns whether objects exist before we happen to identify them as mountains, stars or ammonites. Of course they do. There were trees before they were described as such, and there will still be rocks if everyone decides tomorrow never to call them 'trees' or 'rocks' ever again. The only people who doubt this are those wholesale immaterialists, like Bishop Berkeley (1685–1753), who think that the world exists only in so far as it is actually being perceived.

The other (and, Rorty claims, quite separate) question concerns *how* we identify those objects as mountains, stars or ammonites. The fact of their antecedent existence is no use if we want to ask what their intrinsic essence is, independent of our statements about them. There is nothing describable about stars apart from our descriptions of them. As soon as we find something new about stars, it simply becomes a newly described aspect of stars. Otherwise, there would have to be something about stars which we could *describe* as being intrinsically *undescribable*. Pointing out that this is contradictory amounts merely to the conclusion that 'We can't describe what we can't describe.' And that, of course, is just an uncontroversial, intellectually harmless tautology.

An example might be useful here. Confronted by Berkeley's subjective idealism (one name for the thesis that objects in the external world are products of our perception of them), Samuel Johnson famously kicked a stone, and declared, 'I refute it *thus*.'[7] However difficult, Berkeley's reasoning is impossible to refute on its own terms (how does one prove that the sitting-room persists in its present form while one has left it to put the kettle on, or that England continue playing football with the same dull predictability even when one blinks?). Johnson's point was simple, commonsensical, and also right: rocks exist antecedently to our kicking them. For hardcore idealists, though, his gesture didn't *prove* this as such: his experience of kicking the rock was, after all, another perception. It didn't prove the independent materiality of the world, only that he perceived the requisite sensations pertaining to the kicking of stones. There is a circularity here which 'common sense' finds it difficult to escape from, similar to Descartes' worries about how he could prove to himself that he was not dreaming. Linguistic idealists can employ this circularity by asking us to describe a pre-human world in terms other than those supplied by that thoroughly human creation, language, and then looking on with amusement as we fail to.

Now you might deem this a fairly fatuous intellectual game, or you might take it as indicative of something profound about the relation between (or synthesis of) perception and reality. It is one, shortcutting answer to the question of whether objects have 'intrinsic properties', and if so how much of their properties are projected by us, or by language. More recent species of Berkeley-style arguments might contend, with Nelson Goodman, that while most of us might assume that we construct constellations out of the stars which nature provides, we do in fact construct the stars as well – that everything is brought into being by a particular version of things, and there is no ready-made world waiting for us to come along and label it.[8] Rorty would want to distance himself from this hardcore idealist (or ultra-nominalist) strategy, since he's perfectly happy to admit that stones (and stars) pre-date us. But still he makes trouble for Johnson. For the success of Johnson's stone-kicking 'refutation' of idealism depends itself on him, and his witness Boswell, and Boswell's readers, and you reading this, and me writing it, knowing what a stone is. And this awareness is under a description. It is a product of the ways in which human beings have used marks and noises to describe those antecedently existing objects we know as 'stones'.

There is an echo here of Wittgenstein's argument in the *Philosophical Investigations* that ostensive definition (the sort performed by pointing at something and naming it a 'star') only works against the backdrop of a linguistic practice.[9] Nothing in the relation between pointing finger and object makes for perfect clarity of meaning, perfect understanding of exactly which features of the object are being defined, beyond all possible misinterpretation or without need of further elaboration with more language. This does not, for Rorty, mean that we bring objects into being by describing them, but does mean that our picking them out assumes a sense-giving descriptive background. (One might argue that actually this is fairly trivial, and that Wittgenstein's case is only unsettling to those who thought that knowledge of the world was an entirely atomistic, individualised affair. One could, for instance, grant all this and still insist that 'brute material circumstances affect the power of thought' – that our descriptions do not decide the way things are for us in some one-way process, but rather are themselves influenced by the material aspects of existence. Thus Rorty could arguably be described as an ontological materialist – he believes that there is a real, material world prior to the ways in which we happen to describe it – who is epistemologically nominalist: we can only know what this world is like under a description.)

Well, perhaps. I said above that Rorty would *want* to distance himself from hardcore idealism. Can he? In fact, this is not entirely clear. Certainly, he would concede that even if (as he sees it) there is no independent, extra-descriptive nature of reality, there are still *causal pressures* exerted by reality on us. 'These pressures are under a description, and our description of them will change, but they are pressures none the less' (PSH, 33). Rorty, claiming Wittgenstein and Davidson as corroborative voices, wants us to see the relation of language to world as *merely causal*, rather than also 'fitting', or 'representing', or 'organising' the world.

This, he claims, makes pragmatists neither realist nor idealist: they argue neither that there is a nature of the world independent of our descriptions, nor that we are somehow responsible for the way the world is. Both these assumptions rest on an assumption that either brute physical reality or our own inventiveness must take some sort of determinate priority:

> The way in which a blank takes on the form of the die which stamps it has no analogy to the relation between the truth of a sentence and the event which the sentence is about. When the die hits the blank something causal happens, but as many *facts* are brought into the world as there are languages for describing that causal transaction. . . . To say that we must have respect for facts is just to say that we must, if we are to play a certain language game, play by the rules. To say that we must have respect for unmediated causal forces is pointless. It is like saying that the blank must have respect for the impressed die. The blank has no choice, nor do we. (ORT, 81)

Pragmatists wholeheartedly accept 'the brute, inhuman, causal stubbornness' of physical reality,

But they think this should not be confused with, so to speak, an *intentional* stubbornness, an insistence on being *described in a certain way*, its *own way*. The object can, given a prior agreement on a language game, cause us to hold beliefs, but it cannot suggest beliefs for us to hold. It can only do things which our practices will react to with preprogrammed changes in beliefs. (ORT, 84)

We do not, then, have any choice about how to form beliefs – but we can have a choice about which aspects of physical reality we allow to cause us to form beliefs. There is no *confrontation* here between beliefs and objects, as separate things, but simply a quest for a set of beliefs (caused by physical reality) which is coherent, which works, which makes internal sense. In the quest for such coherence we can, if we are lucky, choose the epistemic community to which we belong, 'whose background beliefs and sense of relevance we share' (RP, 152). We can choose the orientation we take towards physical reality (Berkeley's, for instance, or Johnson's), and which objects to make what Rorty calls, after Daniel Dennett, 'centres of descriptive gravity':

all objects resemble selves in being centres of *descriptive* gravity. Narratives are just a particular form of description – the one employed by novelists and autobiographers – but the sort of thing novelists do is not all that different from the sort of thing logicians, physicists, and moralists do. All these people are weaving or reweaving sets of descriptions of objects. The only general truth we know, and the only one we need to know, about the relations between the objects and the descriptions is that object *X* is what most of the beliefs expressed in statements using the term '*X*' are true of. . . . Like heroines whose stories are told by novelists, and selves whose self-consciousness about their own past character results in the acquisition of a quite different future, objects change as our descriptions of them change. That is to say, their center of descriptive gravity shifts as inquiry proceeds. (TP, 105)

But the trouble here is whether there is really much difference, in practice, between Rorty's position and straightforward linguistic idealism. As a tradition, pragmatism tends to emphasise the primacy of practice, which, it's assumed, delivers answers in a way which old-style metaphysics cannot. The index of successful descriptions is whether they *work*; whether they deliver desired results. There is nothing else to worry about: no 'difference which makes a difference' between the results gained by empirical practice and whatever we might call 'the Truth'. Thus for Rorty it is the practice of describing dinosaurs as dinosaurs which gives dinosaurs causally independent qualities. Outside of this practice, they have no such qualities. So when he says that 'there are objects which are causally independent of human beliefs and desires' (ORT, 101), what he really means is that the redescriptions issuing from human beliefs and desires mark out certain features of dinosaur-hood as causally independent of human beliefs and desires. What difference is there which 'makes a difference' between this position and Berkeley's? What both seem to do, certainly, is reduce the ontological (i.e., what exists), into the epistemological (i.e., what we happen to know, or to have described). Thus there is a sort of identity between descriptions and objects, so that matter, reality, all that might seem discrepant from our descriptions, is collapsed into discourse with no practical remainder. To switch vocabularies: 'content' seems, in practice at any rate, to be collapsed into 'scheme', making 'nature' a simple product of culture. 'Causal independence' is, after all, a contingent, socially constructed notion. To put this differently: practice itself, for Rorty, seems dependent on the prior existence of language. My first distinguishing of the word 'porridge' from my breakfast did not depend on some prior practical engagement with the world, a sense of my own relation to an antecedently existing world which language is, in part, *about*. On Rorty's terms it depended, instead, on the history of previous descriptions of that supposedly 'antecedently existing' world.

But back to his own story. Packaged up with the claim that there is no such thing as an intrinsic quality – nothing which our descriptions can either succeed in grasping, or fail to – comes another: that there is no hard-and-fast distinction to be had between scientific descriptions and non-scientific descriptions, or between talking about the world itself and talking about what we have made up. The problem lies in expecting something general or final to be said about the relationship between language and reality. 'We should just refuse to discuss such topics as "the nature

41

of reference" ' (TP, 90), since, being fixated with the relation between word and world, they are left-over niggles furnished by the scheme/content distinction. Letting go of that distinction means facing up to the pointlessness of asking 'whether there really are mountains or whether it is merely convenient for us to talk about mountains' (TP, 72). Any inquiry depends on mountains being under a description. Describing something is a matter of relating it to other things. We have no choice about this feature of description, although we do have a choice about the descriptions we use.

Our descriptions are not constrained by the 'the truth', then, except in the sense that they are constrained by the norms and priorities of the community in which we happen to be operating – by the sorts of descriptions to which our new descriptions will be relative. But this does not, Rorty claims, mean that we simply do what we like in a world of our own making. That would imply that language is arbitrary. But the tools we use are not random, nor the product of rudderless invention:

> Nor do I think that language is 'an arbitrary system of signs', any more than that the constellations are *arbitrary* arrangements of stars. Given the conditions we live in, they are among the arrangements of stars that it is useful for us to talk about. More generally, given the conditions we live in, the language we use is the obvious way for us to talk. There may be better ways, but they will not be discovered by analyzing the 'conditions of possibility' of present ways . . . They will be discovered by somebody

> proposing a new idiom, its being tried out, and its being
> found to work better than its predecessor. (RP, 125)

This relation of individual creativity to broader social progress is a pivot of Rorty's recent writings. In turn, it pivots on a very particular view of *metaphor*.

METAPHOR AND PROGRESS

> Yeats asked the spirits (whom [*sic*], he believed, were
> dictating *A Vision* to him through his wife's mediumship)
> why they had come. The spirits replied, 'To bring you
> metaphors for poetry.' A philosopher might have
> expected some hard facts about what it was like on the
> other side, but Yeats was not disappointed. (PMN, 359,
> n. 4)

Philosophers, says Rorty, in thrall to the appearance/reality distinction, have worried too much about hard facts – about the real world to which we must be true. His deflationary, utilitarian account of language as a means of coping with the world leads to scrupulous light-mindedness about traditional philosophical topics. This pays off in two distinct ways. It allows us to adopt a pragmatic attitude towards competing descriptions of our circumstances and of the future. Rather than their being entangled in some complex relation to something non-human called Truth, success for these descriptions comes functionally, in the form of meeting social needs. But it also makes room for a Romantic emphasis – thematic through Rorty's writings from the 1960s onwards – on the importance, to individuals and to society at large, of the proposing of new idioms: of *poetry*.

There is a tension here, between Rorty's prizing of poetic free invention, untethered by precedent and convention, and his appeal to more humble, public responsibilities. Rorty seeks to resolve this tension in two ways. As we'll see in the next section, he follows political philosophers of the liberal tradition in insisting that our private poetic pursuits have no public significance unless they harm others. He institutes a split between what J. S. Mill called 'self-regarding' and 'other-regarding' actions: between, roughly speaking, our own business, and that which affects the community of which we are a part. In addition, he gives an account of intellectual progress which explains it as a happy by-product of the accidental coincidence of individual creativity and public need.

Progress for Rorty is change in ways of talking. Vocabularies clash, and get compared: the ones which look bad are discarded, and the ones which look better survive. This depends on unpredictable redescriptions which confound the rules of existing language-games. None of these has everything covered – there is no super-vocabulary, no redescription which redescribes everything at once, which might somehow insure itself against future redescription, against the occurrence of 'the incommunicably and unintelligibly novel' (CP, 8). Neither are there are predescribable rules which could provide advance criteria for the rational reception of every future redescription. The

most fruitful redescriptions tend to start off being *wrong* –
or at any rate downright weird:

> when Christians began saying 'Love is the only law', and
> when Copernicus began saying 'The earth goes round
> the sun', these sentences must have seemed merely
> 'ways of speaking'. Similarly, the sentences 'history is the
> history of class struggle' or 'matter can be changed into
> energy' were, at the first utterance, prima facie false. . . .
> But when the Christians, the Copernicans, the Marxists,
> or the physicists had finished redescribing portions of
> reality in the light of these sentences, we started
> speaking of these sentences as hypotheses, which might
> quite possibly be true. In time, each of these sentences
> became accepted, at least within certain communities of
> inquiry, as *obviously* true. (ORT, 124)

This depiction of the typical way in which our vocabularies
change rests on a very particular view of *metaphor*.

Metaphor has usually been defined as a trope involving a
transfer from literal to figurative meaning. Aristotle defined
it as a sort of deliberate category mistake – 'the application
of an alien name', as he puts it in the *Poetics*, by which one
meaning is created out of another.[10] For Rorty this picture
captures metaphor's intimate relation with the forging of
novel descriptions, but gets the explanation of that relationship wrong by assuming it to be something technical.
He suggests that we think of metaphor 'as a use of language
as yet insufficiently integrated into the language-game to
be captured in a dictionary entry' (HNN, 465). As such, the
distinction between the literal and the metaphorical is not

45

a distinction, or a productive tension, between two sorts of *meaning*, but simply a distinction between familiar and unfamiliar uses of language. On these terms, the literal is that which we can accommodate within existing vocabularies, and the metaphorical is that which stimulates us to come up with a fresh vocabulary. Because they are unfamiliar, uncategorised marks and noises, metaphors are ruleless: they are leaps in the dark. There is no system or structure or rigour linking the conventional with the as-yet unthought, or the expected with the unexpected. Surprises, by definition, aren't predictable.

Rorty invokes Davidson's conclusion that 'metaphors mean what the words, in their most literal sense, mean, and nothing more'[11] to show that it is not their *meaning* which makes metaphors lead to fresh insights, but what they are used to do, and the context in which they are so used:

> In his view, tossing a metaphor into a conversation is like suddenly breaking off the conversation long enough to make a face, or pulling a photograph out of your pocket and displaying it, or pointing at a feature of the surroundings, or slapping your interlocutor's face, or kissing him. Tossing a metaphor into a text is like using italics, or illustrations, or odd punctuation or formats. All of these are ways of producing effects on your interlocutor or your reader, but not ways of conveying a message. (CIS, 18)

On the Davidson–Rorty view of metaphor, the effect of metaphors is *performative* (they describe by *doing* rather than by conveying a semantic content):

> If one had wanted to say something – if one had wanted
> to utter a sentence with a meaning – one would
> presumably have done so. But instead one thought that
> one's aim could be better carried out by other means.
> That one uses familiar words in unfamiliar ways – rather
> than slaps, kisses, pictures, gestures, or grimaces – does
> not show that what one said must have a meaning. An
> attempt to state that meaning would be an attempt to
> find some familiar (that is, literal) use of words – some
> sentence which already had a place in the language
> game – and, to claim that one might just as well have
> said *that*. But the unparaphrasability of metaphor is just
> the unsuitability of any such familiar sentence for one's
> purpose. (CIS, p. 18)

In the sense in which Copernicus and Marx were producing
metaphors, then, there was no way of paraphrasing what
they were saying within the vocabularies already in place.
There was no existing equivalent to their claims. Hence
their *prima facie* falseness.

On Rorty's account, metaphors – for instance, 'rivers
have mouths' – begin life as meaningless precisely because
they appear outside contemporary cognitive horizons. A
metaphor is like a gesture towards something hitherto
unnoticed (perhaps accompanied by a shrug about its real
significance) rather than an explanation of that something.
Nor, naturally, does it help us towards a grasp of true
reality. Just as there is no pre-existent goal of intellectual
inquiry, neither is there any pre-existent goal of the
individual human life, or of the history of a given

community, or of humanity as a whole. These goals are invented, *ad hoc*, on the hoof, in response to the ways in which new, radical, metaphorical ways of speaking happen to link up fruitfully with in-place habits of thought and practice. Because 'poetic, artistic, philosophical, scientific, or political progress results from the accidental convergence of a private obsession with a public need' (CIS, 37), '[t]he proper honour to pay to new, vibrantly alive metaphors, is to help them become dead metaphors as quickly as possible, to rapidly reduce them to the status of tools of social progress' (EHO, 17). Thus, 'Rivers have mouths', 'Love is the only law', 'The earth moves round the sun' or 'All human beings are equal' – useful metaphors all in the history of Western culture – progressed from being 'incommunicably and unintelligibly novel' to being candidates for literal truth.

> Our beliefs were, in the interval, rewoven to make room for these truths – a process which was indistinguishable from the process of changing the meanings of the words used in these sentences in such a way as to make the sentences literally true. (EHO, 13)

Thus, human history can be seen as the history of successive metaphors – or the history of the redescriptions we make in light of a metaphor which, like a kiss or a slap in the face, is something which we take as it strikes us, at the given historical moment, rather than according to cognitive criteria. Thus progress is not *rational* as such, unless by 'rationality' we simply mean that which is consonant with 'the way we normally do things round here', or 'the descriptive conventions and practices of a given historical community'. Whether one can in fact consider redescription as hinging on definitively non-cognitive factors is a moot point; whether 'The earth moves round the sun' was as meaningless, at first utterance, as a slap in the face seems doubtful. The point for Rorty is that 'The earth moves round the sun' was a metaphor which happened to be savoured and retained, and 'The earth is a twinkle in the milkman's eye', *prima facie* on an epistemic par, has simply failed to attain the same consolidation into commonsense usage.

Nietzsche once famously declared truth to be 'metaphors which are worn out and without sensuous power; coins which have lost their pictures and now matter only as metal, only as coins'.[12] This claim determines that the relation between metaphoricity and literalness is simply a temporal one: that there is nothing about '2 plus 2 is 4' that separates it from 'All the world's a stage' except a degree of cultural familiarity with the claim concerned. Crucial for Rorty, too, is that there are no separations of type to be made between self-professedly 'scientific' descriptions and more literary-sounding ones – that 'cultural-economic globalisation', 'the head of the valley' and 'the Big Bang' are all, equally, figurative expressions at various stages on the road to literalness.

Viewed thus, science becomes an aesthetic process. Metaphors trigger redescriptions, which make for progress. Rorty proposes that we 'see the poet, in the generic sense of the maker of new words, the shaper of new languages, as the vanguard of the species' (CIS, 20). But to have constructive, lasting influence on the practices of their community, poets – for all their enterprise – need to exercise a degree of humility in descriptive scope. Most particularly, they should resist 'the urge to make all things new at once, to insist that nothing can change unless everything changes' (RP, 202) – the sort of 'philosophical avant-gardism' which Rorty treats as one of the more harmful intellectual habits. 'No-one,' he says, 'can make sense of the notion of a last commentary, a last discussion note, a good piece of writing which is more than the occasion for a better piece' (CP, 109). This is what separates pragmatists like Rorty from those who seek large-scale solutions to an underlying, perhaps partially obscured, social problem. The difference between them is that between what he calls, respectively, 'utopianism' and 'radicalism':

> Radicals think that there is a basic mistake being made, a mistake deep down at the roots. They think that deep thinking is required to get down to this deep level, and that only there, when all the superstructural appearances have been undercut, can things be seen as they really are. Utopians, though, do not think in terms of mistakes or of depth. They abandon the distinction between superficial appearance and deep reality in favour of the contrast between a painful present and a possibly less painful, dimly seen future. Pragmatists cannot be radical in this sense, but they can be utopians. (TP, p. 214)

This is why redescriptions aren't *theories*: they do not

pretend to assume an elevated critical position, or dig beneath surface appearances. They simply redescribe.

This suspicion of the very idea that contemporary society might be structurally, or deep-rootedly, unjust – together with his oft-stated assumption that American society and values are the best that humankind has managed so far – explains why so much has been written from the political Left about Rorty's apparent breezy complacency, and his apparent readiness to deny all scope for radical social critique. An implicit response (self-coherent, however likely to convince) to the allegation that he is a political conservative comes in *Achieving Our Country*. There he insists that, in fact, the habits and fixations of politically driven theorists often have only a tenuous connection to projects actually making society better. Rorty spends most of *Contingency, Irony, and Solidarity*, too, giving reasons why good poets, good redescribers, adventurous reweavers of their own existing webs of beliefs and desires – like Nietzsche, Proust, Heidegger and Derrida – do not make very good public legislators. Their work makes edifying private reading, but this does not translate into public utility. The same goes for avant-garde political theorists. Their drive for theoretical invention has very little relevance when it comes to progressive politics in the direction of greater human freedom and solidarity.

But they can help with our own self-refashioning as individuals. As reality has no core nature, neither do we. Rorty asks us to see our individual selves, like our community, as narratives in process, as subject to the same continual redescriptions as are our wider social horizons. The self for Rorty is simply the network of beliefs, desires, moods and so on which each of us *is* – and not something separate which *has* those beliefs and desires, which is somehow transcendental or prior to them, and so remains the same throughout our lives, untouched by the reweaving of that network. There is no separate agency which reweaves: rather, the network 'reweaves itself, in response to stimuli such as the new beliefs acquired when, e.g., doors are opened' (ORT, 123). Thus, we are not constrained by the truth of ourselves any more than we are by the truth of the 'external world'. Like the Romantic poets, but without any metaphysical account of our own selfhood, Rorty invests a great deal in our own individual powers of reinvention. The self, like language, is entirely contingent. Like anything else, it can be redescribed.

Thus, just as current social practices, however exploitative or corrupt, cannot be said somehow to be distortively speaking a language at odds with reality, or obscuring the way things really should be, neither is there a core human nature which can be denied by those practices. Unsettling this may be to those of us who had naïvely assumed that slavery was wrong by virtue of what it is to be a human being. But for Rorty his contingency has its progressive upside, in that we need never accept other people's descriptions of ourselves:

> if you find yourself a slave, do not accept your masters'
> descriptions of the real; do not work within the bound-
> aries of their moral universe. Instead, try to create a

reality of your own by selecting aspects of the world that lend themselves to the support of *your* judgement of the worthwhile. (TP, 216)

An 'emancipated' society for Rorty would, in this sense at least, be a society of poets: of people who recognise the contingency of all descriptions, and that 'truth' is something made, not found. 'Emancipation' is not the freeing of a shackled human nature, or the emergence from ignorance into the light of a truer knowledge. It is the substitution of new, better, ways of describing the situation of individuals, groups, and the communities of which they are a part.

A CULTURE OF IRONY AND HOPE

Is Rorty's valorisation of poetry simply élitist and aestheticist, making self and world, social progress and the eradication of human exploitation and starvation into artistic projects for the suitably funded, leisured and aware? He insists not, although it's easy enough to see why the allegation is made.

One worry about Rorty's aestheticisation of inquiry is that it rejects as ill-conceived or useless *any* account of ideology – and thus rejects the very theoretical possibility that certain ideas or beliefs might help bolster existing social relations precisely by distortion and deception. On this score, it simply *cannot* be the case that, say, certain economic interests within society might seek to promulgate self-servingly mendacious accounts of the utility of certain commodities, or the effects on the environment of certain factory emissions, or the conditions under which their overseas workforce are employed. The allegation of any such mendacity would imply that there was some reality there to be so distorted. And

> 'distortion' presupposes a medium of representation which, intruding between us and the object under investigation, produces an appearance that does not correspond to the reality of the object. This representationalism cannot be squared . . . with the pragmatist insistence that truth is not a matter of correspondence to the intrinsic nature of reality. (FID, 98)

A critical approach to culture and society based on any such notion will simply be relying on the same old ocularcentric notion that a portion of reality is, in everyday lived social experience, obscured from our view – that the objects we discuss have some sort of a life of their own external to the language in which we discuss them. It also implies that there is some place outside the horizons of our community from which we can criticise its current norms. For Rorty this is a fundamental error. Faults and misdemeanours in our society can only be addressed from a perspective within its traditions:

> Those who act badly are those who behave contrary to the project which makes us the community we are. . . . The only way we can criticize current social issues is by reference to utopian notions which proceed by taking

> elements in the tradition and showing how unfulfilled
> they are. (FPPP, 2)

Having opened ourselves to the course of conversation, we must accept that criticism and *knowledge* – or at any rate, knowledge on the spectatorial model – need have no connection. For their part, having dropped all hope of finding changeless, rock-solid certainty, theorists should take a lesson from Dewey: 'philosophy can proffer only hypotheses, and . . . these hypotheses are of value only as they render men's minds more sensitive to the life about them'. 'In a fully temporalized intellectual world,' says Rorty, 'contributing to such sensitivity would be just as respectable a goal for an academic discipline as contributing to knowledge' (RP, 205). Rorty approvingly cites Vaclav Havel's dictum, 'Hope is not prognostication' as 'substituting groundless hope for theoretical insight' (TP, 236). It exemplifies the recognition that

> Our identification with our community – our society, our
> political tradition, our intellectual heritage – is heightened when we see this community as *ours* rather than
> *nature's*, *shaped* rather than *found*, one among many
> which men have made. In the end, pragmatists tell us,
> what matters is our loyalty to other human beings
> clinging together against the dark, not our hope of
> getting things right. [O]ur glory is in our participation in
> fallible and transitory human projects, not in our obedience to permanent nonhuman constraints. (CP, 166)

Returning to the distinction mentioned earlier, we can take

loyalty here as a *horizontal* rather than a *vertical* relationship. Proceeding vertically, we search for something determinate underlying the indeterminate: a hook upon which to hang our prognoses. This search might go 'downwards' (seeking something deep – as in Marx's metaphor of the economic base ultimately determining the political superstructure), or 'upwards' (seeking something transcendent, as in Christianity's appeal to the word of God). Relying only on loyalty and hope, we make no such vertical moves to justify our descriptions.

What Rorty calls (in *Consequences of Pragmatism*) a 'post-Philosophical culture' is characterised by an ongoing process of description and redescription. As he says, 'The kind of name-dropping, rapid shifting of context, and unwillingness to stay for an answer which this culture encourages runs counter to everything that a professionalized academic discipline stands for' (CP, 65). What enables us to make criticism of claims made within our culture and our inherited standards of truth is not appeals, vertically, to some ahistorical standard or regulative idea, but 'concrete alternative suggestions – suggestions about how to redescribe what we are talking about' (TF, 634). 'If there is social hope it lies in the imagination – in people describing a future in terms which the past did not use' (EHO, 186). Our redescriptions will inevitably involve contrast-effects with cultures other than that to which we owe our loyalties and convictions – distinctions between what 'we' believe and other, less savoury options – since it is *only* our cultural situatedness, in the absence of any 'vertical' appeal, which can provide an available ground for those affinities:

There is no 'ground' for such loyalties and convictions save the fact that the beliefs and desires and emotions which buttress them overlap those of lots of other members of the group with which we identify for purposes of moral or political deliberations, and the further fact that these are *distinctive* features of that group, features which it uses to construct its self-image through contrasts with other groups. ... Nations or churches or movements are, on this view, shining historical examples not because they reflect rays emanating from a higher source, but because of contrast-effects – comparisons with other, worse communities.

. . . the moral justification of the institutions and practices of one's group – e.g., of the contemporary bourgeoisie – is mostly a matter of historical narratives (including scenarios about what is likely to happen in certain future contingencies), rather than of philosophical metanarratives. The principal backup for historiography is not philosophy but the arts, which serve to develop and modify a group's self-image by, for example, apotheosizing its heroes, diabolizing its enemies, mounting dialogues among its members, and refocusing its attention.

. . . we need not presuppose a *persistent* 'we', a trans-historical metaphysical subject, in order to tell stories of progress. The only 'we' we need is a local and temporary one: 'we' means something like 'us twentieth-century Western social democrats'. (ORT, 200, 214)

But redescriptions like those that poets apply to themselves would, transferred to society at large, mean an echo of the 'urge to make all things new at once'. The Romantic ideal of self-invention works fine for individuals, but is a bad model for society. *Contingency, Irony, and Solidarity*, a decade after *Philosophy and the Mirror of Nature*, made a central point of the idea that philosophically iconoclastic theorists like Nietzsche and Derrida make works suitable only for *private* consumption rather than constructive *public* dissemination. Precisely because they strip us of all remaining metaphysical urges – so demonstrating (at least on Rorty's pragmatist reading) the sheer contingency of all ideas of morality, progress, justice and the like – they contribute to the private inculcation of an advanced 'ironist' stance, but not to progressive politics. 'Ironism' derives from an awareness of the power of redescription. Rorty defines the figure of the ironist as the sort of person who 'does not think that [one's] vocabulary is closer to reality than others'', who sees 'one's language, one's conscience, one's morality, and one's highest hopes as contingent products, as literalizations of what once were accidentally produced metaphors' (CIS, 73, 61).

This sort of self-identity makes for the ideal citizenship of what Rorty proposes as 'the ideal liberal state'. The citizens of Rorty's utopia would be *liberal ironists*: 'people who combined commitment [to liberal values like freedom, solidarity, and the avoidance of cruelty] with a sense of the contingency of their own commitment' (CIS, 61). Rather than seeking to 'make all things new at once', the socially minded ideal citizen would live in the sort of 'lightly-

sketched future' which might inspire her 'confused, uto-
pian, unscientific, petty bourgeois followers' to 'make the
actual future better for the rest of us' (EHO, 183). The self-
image of Western liberal capitalist democracies is, Rorty
argues, perfectly adequate to this task of ongoing adjustment in response to lightly sketched futures which chime
with the values embodied in that self-image. But it is not,
by and large, political or legal *theory* which is responsible for
this adjustment:

> [the recent West is] a culture often said, with excellent
> reason, to be racist, sexist, and imperialist. But it is of
> course also a culture which is very *worried* about being
> racist, sexist, and imperialist, as well as about being
> Eurocentric, parochial, and intellectually intolerant. It is a
> culture which has become very conscious of its capacity
> for murderous intolerance and thereby perhaps more
> wary of intolerance, more sensitive to the desirability of
> diversity than any other of which we have record. I have
> been suggesting that we Westerners owe this conscious-
> ness and this sensitivity more to our novelists than to our
> philosophers or our poets. (EHO, p. 81)

One might interject here that American culture is by no
means uniformly, or even predominantly, beset by such
worries, and struggle to imagine Ronald Reagan or Bill
Gates flagellating themselves over the ethical implications
of US imperialism. But it is worth noting that the gist of
Rorty's point here does have a longer pedigree. David Hume
(1711–76), as have many since, insisted that ethical actions
are, and are better, based on feelings (like sympathy) than

on rational principles. In a way, Rorty just restates this point. The moral vocabulary of the 'we' to which we are allied is the product of sentiment not reason, affect not effect. Sentiment can motivate; reason cannot. Human solidarity, a defining aim for 'we social democrats' (or, more regularly, 'we liberals'), has no vertical foundations to make every human being somehow worthy of respect *qua* human being. Rather, 'humanity' becomes a flexible, sentimentally driven notion dependent on how far we can extend our sense of 'us' – dependent upon noticing similarities between 'our' practices and those of other cultures hitherto assumed to be different.

By way of example, Rorty invokes journalism from the 1990s conflict in the former Yugoslavia to demonstrate that those committing acts of sheer sadism in such cases do not see themselves as violating human rights; 'For they are not doing these things to fellow human beings, but to *Muslims*. They are not being inhuman, but rather are discriminating between true humans and pseudo-humans. They are making the same sort of distinction that the Crusaders made between humans and infidel dogs' – or, for that matter, that of Thomas Jefferson, slave-owning drafter of the American constitution's declaration that 'all men are created equal', who convinced himself that black people are not really *human* (TP, 167). Note that Rorty cannot insist here that the Crusaders or Jefferson got things *wrong* – only that the limited scope of the human 'we' to which they belonged should be expanded by redescription.[13] (You do not have to be a pragmatist to endorse the thesis that our political and moral beliefs and assumptions are embedded in our practical engagement with each other and with the world. But there is a sizeable jump from this stance to Rorty's thoroughgoing ethnocentrism: the claim that the sedimented, literalised values of the community of which we are a part are, however parochial, all we have conversational recourse to, and that, consequently, we should 'divide the human race into the people to whom one must justify one's beliefs and the others' (ORT, 32).)

And because this sort of redescription is exactly the sort which provokes a sentimental sense of human solidarity in us, this is a job better done by novelists, docu-drama makers, comic-book creators or journalists than by philosophers. Systematic, rule-providing theories of justice might have a certain beauty, but they are of little use when it comes down to the messy business of muddling through to a fairer society:

> A society which took its moral vocabulary from novels rather than from ontotheological or ontico-moral treatises would not ask itself questions about human nature, the point of human existence, or the meaning of human life. Rather, it would ask itself what we can do to get along with each other, how we can arrange things so that everyone's right to be understood has a better chance of being gratified (EHO, p. 78)

– a 'right to be understood' which is itself, of course, the product of 'our' own vocabulary, and is extendable as far as the human constituency which we have succeeded in describing as 'us'.

CONCLUSION

The 'cash value' (to speak, when in Rome, in appropriately pragmatist terms) of Rorty's propositions about the relations between language, world and society is that the question of which descriptions 'win out', and so 'stick', becomes a social affair. This leads to what for many is the most problematic aspect of Rorty's thought: its apparent reduction of all critical criteria to simple consensus and convention – its claim that objectivity is only, simply, intersubjective agreement. Rorty's post-Philosophical culture would welcome fresh redescriptions – but these are to be evaluated only in terms of current, sedimented 'common sense'. This has led to frequent charges of outright relativism. Like the Cretan declaring that all Cretans are liars, relativism is usually regarded as being a self-contradictory position: from what *absolute* standpoint does one make the judgement that *all* judgements are *relative*? It also seems to suggest that flatly contradictory judgements can both be true simultaneously when made within different cultural circumstances. Whatever 'truth' is, it cannot be stretched to simultaneously cover fifty-three radically incompatible conclusions. But aside from problems of non-contradictory definition, the spectre of outright relativism seems to be the spectre of the conclusion that the assumptions behind different practices (neo-Nazi, genocidal or humanitarian) are, at a deep level, on a par, and that minority opinions are, by definition, wrong. Intersubjective approval has been granted to some pretty dubious theses. Does that make them 'true', or acceptable? Some cultures have deemed it true that certain races are fit only for slavery or extermination. Can't we claim that they are *wrong* about this in any sense stronger than 'that's not what we think around here'? It seems any card-carrying relativist would have to answer 'no'.

Which is one reason why relatively few people call themselves relativists. Is Rorty one? He has well-rehearsed responses to the charge. A crucial, if unsurprising, move he makes is to suggest that the problem of relativism arises only if one takes the traditional philosophical agenda seriously in the first place. The trouble comes from thinking of rationality as involving a neutral set of publicly available criteria which, applied correctly, will settle all arguments:

> Only someone who did think of rationality in this way would dream of suggesting that 'true' means something different in different societies. For only such a person could imagine that there was anything to pick out to which one might make 'true' relative. Only if one shares the logical positivists' idea that we all carry around things called 'rules of language' which regulate what we say when, will one suggest that there is no way to break out of one's culture. (ORT, 25–6)

And only if one worries about the nature of a true, non-human world will one be worried about our position relative to it. Similarly:

'Relativism' is the view that every belief on a certain topic, or perhaps about *any* topic, is as good as every other. No one holds this view. Except for the occasional cooperative freshman, one cannot find anyone who says that two incompatible opinions on an important topic are equally good. ... [T]he real issue is not between people who think one view as good as another and people who do not. It is between those who think our culture, or purpose, or intuitions cannot be supported except conversationally, and people who still hope for other sorts of support. (CP, 166–7)

Two levels of claim are operating here. Firstly, 'ethnocentrism' (defined, again, as the idea that we are culturally situated beings who must, when evaluating competing claims, work by our own lights) is not the same as relativism (the thesis that alternative cultures operate by radically incommensurable, or untranslatable, rules). For if you believe that 'our culture, or purpose, or intuitions' can only be supported conversationally, then (unless you think that conversation takes place under the aegis of pre-ordained rules) there is nothing which can make our culture *in principle* irreconcilable with another. 'To think otherwise,' says Rorty, 'is the Cartesian fallacy of seeing axioms where there are only shared habits, of viewing statements which summarize such practices as if they reported constraints enforcing such practices' (ORT, 26). In other words, it is a symptom of the scheme/content distinction: an insistence that there must be conceptual corollaries of empirical differences. Thus nothing divides up different worldviews or practices according to different sets of rules, thereby making it logically impossible to reconcile them. It's just that, in seeking intercultural (or indeed intersubjective) agreement, we start from where we are, rather than assuming some presuppositionless vantage point.

Secondly, and less predictably, there is the claim that 'true' means the same in all cultures. Rorty can make this sort of claim precisely because he doesn't think that truth is the sort of thing about which it is useful to have a theory. As with 'good', or 'agreeable', 'true' in any culture is just the sort of compliment that one pays to a proposition to which one consents. Thus, in a footnote, Rorty draws the seemingly uncharacteristic conclusion that:

> 'Slavery is absolutely wrong' has always been true – even in periods when this sentence would have sounded crazy to everyone concerned, even the slaves (TP, 225, n. 42)

– a claim that he can quite happily make because the truth of that statement has nothing to do with the antecedently existing reality of slavery's wrongness, and everything to do with our approval of it.

> 'Truth' is not the name of a power that eventually wins through; it is just the nominalization of an approbative adjective. (TP, 225–6)

All pragmatists need to do is claim that this sentence is not *made* true by something other than the beliefs we'd use to support it. This is not, as far as Rorty is concerned, a momentary rush of unethnocentrist blood to the head. All that he is saying is that a truth is a truth: that truth is 'eternal and enduring' (RP, 144), that true sentences are always true. On his terms, this is no different to saying that goodness is eternal and enduring. The important thing is that in neither 'truth' nor 'goodness' is there any determinate relation between concept and empirical reality. 'Truth' is simply not all that important beyond its status, at the conversational level, as one of the heartiest ways in which we can commend a sentence.

Does this make sense? Does it rob 'truth' of all special significance? Does 'slavery is wrong', if 'true' in these terms, offer purchase or significance or critical bite? Does this matter? Not greatly to Rorty, who would be quite happy if 'Truth, theories of' became a cobwebbed curiosity in dictionaries of that old-time discipline known to future intellectual historians as 'Philosophy'. But one does not have to have any interest in preserving the cultural practice of purist philosophy for its own sake to suspect that this has huge social (indeed, practical) implications. Hence – in addition to the offence he has caused philosophers who take 'traditional' problems of mind and knowledge more seriously than he does – his even-handed irritation of those whose aim is radical social change and those who most strongly resist it.

This is explained by the claims Rorty makes about the role of redescription, which suggest *both* that, in terms of knowledge-claims, anything goes (or that anything, at any rate, can be made to look true or false by being redescribed) *and* that truth and social norms are derivable only from mainstream consensus belief. Do these claims fit with each other? The crucial point becomes: does *anything* constrain or limit our redescriptions in terms of their power to make the world different – i.e., is Rorty indeed, in effect, despite his protestations, a linguistic idealist? Is the cash value of his declaration that 'there is no answer to a redescription save a re-re-redescription' (CIS, 80) a conclusion that all reality is not just *under* a description, but a *product* of it? If all our knowledge-claims are descriptions, and descriptions can be validated only in terms of the ends they serve, does it matter if those ends themselves can be validated only by further descriptions? These are sticky, stubborn questions, adhering to anyone to whom criticism of social practices has any importance, as well as those concerned with the nature (if such indeed there is) of language, communication, truth or knowledge. Whether or not Rorty's answers dig Philosophy's grave, his questions, deep and nuanced, haunt the age.

SOURCES

1. 'The hundred most influential books since the war', *Times Literary Supplement*, 6 October 1995.

2. Plato, *The Republic*, Part VII, § 7 (pp. 316–25 in Desmond Lee's translation, Harmondsworth: Penguin Books, 1955; orig. c. 375 BC).

3. René Descartes, *Discourse on Method and the Meditations*, translated by F. E. Sutcliffe (Harmondsworth: Penguin Books, 1968; orig. 1641), pp. 100, 103.

4. William James, *Pragmatism* (Mineola, NY: Dover, 1995; orig. 1907), p. 30.

5. See Donald Davidson, 'On the Very Idea of a Conceptual Scheme', in his *Inquiries into Truth and Interpretation* (Oxford: Clarendon Press, 1984).

6. Ludwig Wittgenstein, *Philosophical Investigations*, 3rd edition, translated by G. E. M. Anscombe (Oxford: Blackwell, 1974; orig. 1953), § 11, p. 6.

7. James Boswell, *The Life of Samuel Johnson* (Ware: Wordsworth, 1999; orig. 1791), p. 238.

8. See the pieces of Goodman and others collected in Peter J. McCormick (ed.), *Starmaking: Realism, Anti-Realism, and Irrealism* (Cambridge, Mass.: MIT Press, 1996).

9. Wittgenstein, *Philosophical Investigations*, § 27–30, pp. 13–15.

10. Aristotle, *Poetics*, translated by S. H. Butcher (Mineola, NY: Dover, 1997; orig. c. 330 BC), p. 41.

11. Davidson, 'What Metaphors Mean', in his *Inquiries into Truth and Interpretation*, p. 245.

12. Friedrich Nietzsche, 'On Truth and Lie in an Extra-Moral Sense', in Walter Kaufman (ed.), *The Portable Nietzsche* (New York: The Viking Press, 1954), pp. 46–7.

13. For an extended discussion of this aspect of Rorty's thought see Norman Geras, *Solidarity in the Conversation of Humankind: The Ungroundable Liberalism of Richard Rorty* (London: Verso, 1995), especially chapters 2 and 3.

ABBREVIATIONS

Works by Rorty referred to in the text

PCL 'Pragmatism, Categories, and Language', *Philosophical Review* 70, 1961, pp. 197–223.

LT (editor) *The Linguistic Turn: Essays in Philosophical Method*, 2nd edition with two new essays (Chicago: University of Chicago Press, 1992; orig. 1967).

PMN *Philosophy and the Mirror of Nature* (Oxford: Blackwell, 1980).

FPPP 'From Philosophy to Post-Philosophy', interview with Wayne Hudson and Wim van Reijen, *Radical Philosophy* 32, Autumn 1982.

CP *Consequences of Pragmatism* (Minneapolis: University of Minnesota Press, 1982).

PP 'Philosophy without Principles', *Critical Inquiry* 11 (1985), p. 461.

HNN 'The Higher Nominalism in a Nutshell: A Reply to Henry Staten', *Critical Inquiry* 12 (1986), pp. 462–6.

FE 'Foucault and Epistemology', in David C. Hoy (ed.), *Foucault: A Critical Reader* (Oxford: Blackwell, 1986).

CIS *Contingency, Irony, and Solidarity* (Cambridge: Cambridge University Press, 1989).

PAR 'Introduction: Pragmatism as Anti-Representationalism', in John P. Murphy, *Pragmatism from Peirce to Davidson* (Boulder: Westview Press, 1990).

TF 'Truth and Freedom: A Reply to Thomas McCarthy', *Critical Inquiry* 16 (Spring 1996), pp. 633–43.

ORT *Objectivity, Relativism, and Truth: Philosophical Papers Volume 1* (Cambridge: Cambridge University Press, 1991).

EHO *Essays on Heidegger and Others: Philosophical Papers Volume 2* (Cambridge: Cambridge University Press, 1991).

FID 'Feminism, Ideology, and Deconstruction: A Pragmatist View', *Hypatia* vol. 8, no. 2 (Spring 1993), pp. 96–103.

RP Herman J. Saatkamp, Jr (ed.), *Rorty and Pragmatism: The Philosopher Replies to his Critics* (Nashville: Vanderbilt University Press, 1995).

DP Simon Critchley, Jacques Derrida, Ernesto Laclau and Richard Rorty, *Deconstruction and Pragmatism*, ed. Chantal Mouffe (London and New York: Routledge, 1996).

SSB 'Something to Steer By' (review of *John Dewey and the High Tide of American Liberalism* by Alan Ryan), *London Review of Books*, 20 June 1996, pp. 7–9.

AOC *Achieving Our Country: Leftist Thought in Twentieth Century America* (Cambridge, Mass.: Harvard University Press, 1998).

TP *Truth and Progress: Philosophical Papers Volume 3* (Cambridge: Cambridge University Press, 1998).

PSH *Philosophy and Social Hope* (Harmondsworth: Penguin Books, 1999).

I'd like to thank Christopher Norris for his comments on the first draft of this book.